Seasons

Spring

Siân Smith

Heinemann
LIBRARY

www.heinemannlibrary.co.uk
Visit our website to find out more information about Heinemann Library books.

To order:
☎ Phone +44 (0) 1865 888066
🖷 Fax +44 (0) 1865 314091
🖳 Visit www.heinemannlibrary.co.uk

Heinemann Library is an imprint of Capstone Global Library Limited, a company incorporated in England and Wales having its registered office at 7 Pilgrim Street, London, EC4V 6LB – Registered company number: 6695582

Heinemann is a registered trademark of Pearson Education Limited, under licence to Capstone Global Library Limited

Text © Capstone Global Library Limited 2009
First published in hardback in 2009
The moral rights of the proprietor have been asserted.

Edited by Rebecca Rissman, Charlotte Guillain, and Siân Smith
Designed by Joanna Hinton-Malivoire
Picture research by Elizabeth Alexander and Sally Claxton
Production by Duncan Gilbert
Originated by Heinemann Library
Printed and bound in China by South China Printing Company Ltd

ISBN 978 0 431 19278 9
13 12 11 10 09
10 9 8 7 6 5 4 3 2 1

British Library Cataloguing in Publication Data
Smith, Siân
 Spring. - (Seasons)
 1. Spring - Juvenile literature
 I. Title
 508.2

Acknowledgements
The author and publisher are grateful to the following for permission to reproduce copyright material: ©Alamy pp.**8** (Adam Burton), **11** (Alistair Heap), **7** (Andrew Cowin), **21** (Arco Images GmbH), **17** (Nature Online); ©Corbis pp.**16**, **10** (amanaimages/Steve Cole), **20** (Brakefield Photo/Brand X), **04 br** (Image100), **14, 23 top** (John Aikins), **18** (Julie Habel), **9** (Mark Karrass), **5** (Momatiuk-Eastcott), **13, 23 middle top** (Papilio/Steve Austin), **19** (Sygma/Andre Fatras), **04 tl** (Zefa/Roman Flury); ©Getty Images pp.**12, 23 bottom** (Bob Thomas), **04 tr** (Floria Werner); ©iStockphoto.com pp.**6, 23 middle bottom** (Bojan Tezak), **04 bl** (Inga Ivanova); ©Photodisc p.**15** (Lifelife/Andrew Ward); ©Shutterstock p.**22** (Katerina Havelkova).

Cover photograph of purple and yellow crocus reproduced with permission of ©Gap Photos Ltd (J S Sira). Back cover photograph reproduced with permission of ©Corbis (Mark Karrass).

Every effort has been made to contact copyright holders of material reproduced in this book. Any omissions will be rectified in subsequent printings if notice is given to the publishers.

Contents

What is spring?

spring

summer

autumn

winter

There are four seasons every year.

Spring is one of the four seasons.

When is spring?

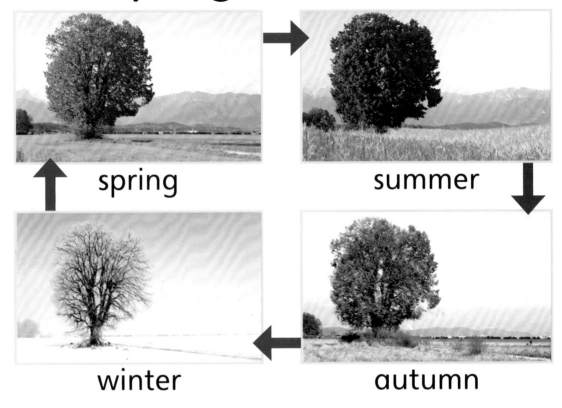

spring

summer

winter

autumn

The four seasons follow a pattern.

Spring comes after winter.

The weather in spring

It can be warm in spring.

It can rain in spring.

What can we see in spring?

In spring we can see people
in raincoats.

In spring we can see people in boots.

seed

In spring we can see people planting seeds.

bud

In spring we can see buds.

In spring we can see blossom.

In spring we can see flowers.

In spring we can see new plants
starting to grow.

In spring we can see new leaves
starting to grow.

In spring we can see eggs in nests.

In spring we can see chicks in nests.

In spring we can see baby animals.

In spring we can see hedgehogs waking up.

Which season comes next?

Which season comes after spring?

Picture glossary

 **blossom** flowers on trees

 **bud** part of a plant. Leaves or flowers come out of buds.

 **pattern** happening in the same order

 **seed** plants make seeds. Seeds grow into new plants.

Index

Notes for parents and teachers
Before reading
Talk to the children about the four seasons of the year: spring, summer, autumn, winter.
Ask the children when their birthdays are and tell them which season their birthday falls in.
Explain that spring is the season when things start to grow after the cold period of winter.
Listen to a few minutes of *Spring* from Vivaldi's *Four Seasons*. Tell the children to close their
eyes and think about the following images of spring: buds and blossom growing on trees,
baby lambs playing in the fields, spring flowers in the parks and gardens.

After reading
• Make a seed head. Collect plastic mini yogurt pots and wash them thoroughly. Fill each
  pot with potting compost three quarters full. Sprinkle mustard cress seeds into the soil
  and then moisten the soil with cold water. Using gummed paper cut out eyes, a nose and
  a mouth and stick these on the pots. Leave the pots on the window ledge in the sun. Add
  water if the soil dries out. Watch as the "hair" grows.
• Learn this poem with hand actions: A little seed for me to sow (mime holding up a seed),
  A little earth to make it grow (cup the other hand to suggest it holds soil), A little hole, a
  little pat (mime making a dip in the soil, placing the seed and covering it), A little wish, and
  that is that (interlink fingers), A little sun (open arms, palms upward); a little shower (use
  fingers to suggest falling rain), A little while ... and then a flower (use opening hands to
  suggest a growing flower).